Ap
2001

Dear
Jonathan,
Yes, it really happened. This is
not science fiction. Oh, the marvels
you will witness in your lifetime!
Happy decade — 10 years Wow!.

Love,
Aunt Irene, Uncle Hal
David &
Jenny

IN SPACE

AUTHOR: MICHAEL JOHNSTONE ✪ CONSULTANT: DOUGLAS MILLARD

DEAR READER,

THE STORY OF OUR ADVENTURE IN SPACE IS NOT SIMPLY A MODERN TALE. SINCE ANCIENT TIMES, MEN AND WOMEN HAVE LOOKED UP INTO THE SKY, WONDERED AT WHAT THEY SAW, AND DREAMED OF TRAVELING TO THE STARS.

THAT'S WHY, AS WELL AS TELLING THE ENTHRALLING STORY OF THE RUSSIAN AND AMERICAN SPACE RACE THIS CENTURY, WE GO RIGHT BACK IN TIME TO LOOK AT THE COLORFUL CHARACTERS THROUGH HISTORY WHO RISKED RIDICULE AND SOMETIMES THEIR LIVES WHEN THEY PUT FORWARD THE IDEAS THAT STARTED OUR JOURNEY INTO SPACE.

IN COMPILING THIS BOOK, WE HAVE HIGHLIGHTED A FEW ASTOUNDING HUMAN ACHIEVEMENTS. THE RESULT IS A SELECTION OF STUNNING STORIES OF COURAGE, HOPE, AND ADVENTURE. WE'VE HAD A LOT OF FUN SELECTING THESE STORIES, AND WE HOPE YOU'LL ENJOY READING THEM AS MUCH AS WE'VE ENJOYED CHOOSING THEM FOR YOU.

THE EDITOR IN CHIEF

Michael Johnstone

A NOTE FROM OUR PUBLISHER
As we all know, newspapers didn't really exist when people first looked at the stars.
But if they had, we're sure everyone would have been reading *The History News*!
We hope you enjoy it.

Candlewick Press

CANDLEWICK PRESS
CAMBRIDGE, MASSACHUSETTS

CONTENTS

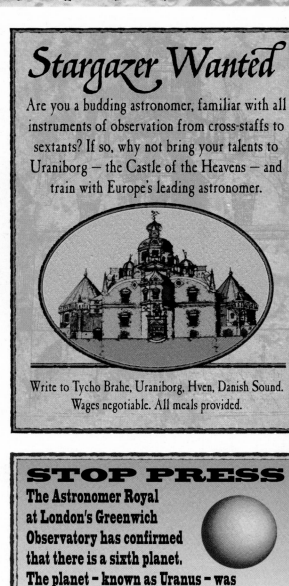

As long as 2,500 years ago, the Ancient Greeks looked at the world around them and tried to make sense of what they saw. By asking questions and suggesting possible answers they came up with many ideas that tried to explain how the Moon, the stars, and the planets move around us in the sky. In this way, the Greeks formed a view of the universe generally accepted for 1,500 years.

STARGAZING: The Ancient Greeks increased their understanding of the universe by watching how the Moon and stars moved in the night sky.

OUT OF THIS WORLD!

Illustrated by SYDNEY COULDRIDGE

ASTRONOMER Ptolemy's book *The Great Astronomical System* drew a picture of the universe that went unchallenged for 1,400 years. When it first appeared in A.D. 145, *The History News* hailed it as a work of genius.

IN HIS BRILLIANT new book, Claudius Ptolemy has established beyond a doubt that our home, Earth, sits at the center of the universe, with the Sun and the other planets revolving around it.

Of course, this notion is not a new one. Back in 560 B.C., that great Greek thinker Pythagoras had already come to the same conclusion. And Ptolemy's theory that the stars and planets are fixed to solid spheres that move around the Earth isn't original either. Five hundred years ago, around 340 B.C., famous Greek philosopher Aristotle talked of these "heavenly spheres."

So how does a book of second-hand ideas justify being called "brilliant"?

The fact is this talented astronomer has studied and combined the ideas into one perfectly complete view of our universe.

A GENIUS OF OBSERVATION

What's more, Ptolemy has even drawn a model of the universe, showing exactly how the Sun, the Moon, and the planets are positioned around the Earth. He has been able to do this by noting down how and to what degree the planets move across our sky. And he has included tables of these movements in his book so it will be possible to calculate the position of the Sun, the Moon, and the five planets—Mars, Mercury, Venus, Saturn, and Jupiter. Altogether it's quite an accomplishment —no wonder Ptolemy is being regarded as the greatest astronomer who has ever lived!

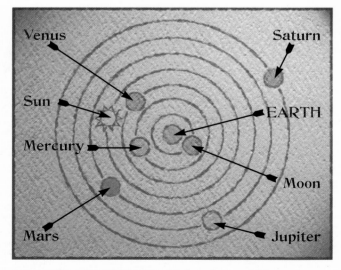

MAPPING THE HEAVENS: Ptolemy's view of the universe.

FOLLOWING THE COLLAPSE OF THE ROMAN EMPIRE IN THE A.D. 400S, EUROPE HAD PLUNGED INTO THE PERIOD KNOWN AS THE DARK AGES. GREEK LEARNING WAS SLOWLY LOST, APART FROM SOME ARABIC TRANSLATIONS OF PTOLEMY'S BOOK THAT STILL EXISTED IN ISLAMIC LANDS. BY THE 1450S, WORKS BY PTOLEMY AND OTHER GREEK THINKERS WERE AT LAST REDISCOVERED BY THE WEST AND TRANSLATED INTO ENGLISH, HERALDING A NEW AGE OF ASTRONOMY.

MOVING HEAVEN AND EARTH

Illustrated by ROD AND KIRA JOSEY

THIS NEWSPAPER IS never slow when it comes to uncovering hot news items. But in 1543, when we talked to a dying priest, not even we could have anticipated the Earth-shattering revelations he'd make.

THE CHURCH teaches that God created the universe with the Earth at its center. After spending more than half a century observing the stars, a Polish priest by the name of Nicolaus Copernicus believes the Church may actually be wrong!

In an interview on his deathbed, he revealed how he came to this shocking conclusion.

As a student, he had read *Almagest*, Ptolemy's *The Great Astronomical System*. This is the standard textbook on astronomy and one of the few that have been translated from the Greek.

He also read the works of other ancient Greek astronomers. And, to his great surprise, he discovered that around 300 B.C. a man called Aristarchus of Samos had written a theory that conflicted with that of the great Ptolemy. Far from believing that the Earth lies at the center of the universe as Ptolemy did many years later, this man thought that the Earth travels around the Sun! Intrigued by these two opposing theories, Copernicus was determined to learn the truth.

In 1512, Copernicus was appointed priest to the small Polish town of Frauenburg, where he has lived ever since. He found that the peacefulness of his surroundings provided a perfect setting for his astronomical studies.

AT THE CENTER OF IT ALL

As we continued to talk, it became clear that the task he had set himself—to discover the truth about the universe—had become as much a part of his life as his duties as a priest.

He explained to me that the more he studied the movements of the planets in the night sky and tried to match them with the theories in Ptolemy's book, the more convinced he became that the great astronomer had been wrong. He felt

THE SUN KING: A century after Copernicus's death, astronomers draw Sun-centered maps of the heavens.

certain that the object that sits at the center of the universe is the Sun and not the Earth. Copernicus concluded, therefore, that the Earth itself is merely another planet which also circles the Sun.

A MAN IN TWO MINDS

I admit that although at first his theory seemed preposterous, all of the arguments he gave me in support of it were very convincing. And when he confided in me that, in 1530, he had written the results of his research in a secret book, which he called *De Revolutionibus*, I asked him why he had not published it. This question was met with a weary shake of the head.

Respecting the old man's wishes, *The History News* promised not to report the interview until after his death. Sadly, we have just learned that Copernicus has died. To print the story can't do him any harm now, and the public deserves to know the astonishing truth about his discoveries.

It seems that in the days before his death, Copernicus's friends at last persuaded him to give his permission to have the book published. Experts who have read it are already proclaiming *De Revolutionibus*, which contains charts and tables in support of his theories, a work of pure genius.

It may take some time for people to catch on to this whole new way of looking at the universe, but one thing is for certain: we haven't heard the last of Copernicus's revolutionary views. ☎

KEPLER CRACKS IT!

Illustrated by MIKE WHITE

COPERNICUS'S THEORY may have sounded the death knell for the Ptolemaic view of the universe, but it was mathematician Johan Kepler who hammered the final nail into its coffin. In 1609, *The History News* ran this report on Kepler's mind-blowing discoveries.

PICTURE PERFECT: Kepler draws a true picture of planetary motion.

IN 1600, WHEN the mathematician Johan Kepler moved to Prague to become assistant to the astronomer Tycho Brahe, it proved to be a momentous meeting of great minds.

Kepler knew that Brahe had spent years compiling the most detailed list of planetary motions that had ever been produced, and he was eager to use it.

As it turned out, they had only a year of working together before Brahe's death in 1601. But Kepler was already on the brink of an important discovery.

He had studied Brahe's writing closely and made drawings of the paths of the planets —their orbits—based on the calculations Brahe had noted. But to his amazement, the shapes he came up with were not circular, as he had been led to believe, at all.

After long hours of observing the planetary movements for himself, the true picture began to unfold. Instead of following a circular path around the Sun, the planets' orbits are elliptical, or oval! What's more, he realized that the nearer the planets are to the Sun, the faster they are likely to travel.

Having recently published a book about his findings, Kepler is only too aware of the shock that his discovery will cause to all those astronomers who have absolute faith in Copernicus's theory. They must now accept that the great man only got it partly right. However, thanks to Kepler, it's now possible to predict exactly where in the sky a planet will be on any day, in any year, until the end of time. ☎

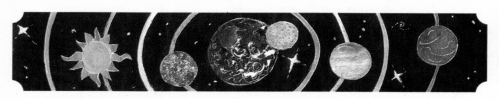
CHURCH OUTLAWS COPERNICAN VIEW

FOR YEARS AFTER his death, Copernicus's book was read only by astronomers. But by 1600, his ideas began to reach a wide audience, and the Christian Church went on the warpath against it, as this letter from the head of the Church, the Pope, to our editor reveals.

From the office of Pope Paul V

Rome, March 30, 1616

Dear Editor,

It has come to our attention that your newspaper has made mention of the theory proposed by Nicolaus Copernicus that the Sun sits at the center of the universe and that the planets, including the Earth, revolve around it.

May we remind you that these views, as expressed in his book *De Revolutionibus*, directly contradict the teachings of the Church, which uphold the Bible's view of creation. The Book of Genesis states quite clearly that the Earth, not the Sun, is at the center of the universe.

As of today, the offending publication has been placed on our Index of Forbidden Books. Support for the book shall be treated as heresy, a crime which carries heavy penalties ~ even death ~ as we are sure you must be aware.

We feel certain that you will make amends for your error and never again print statements in your newspaper in support of the Copernican view.

Yours in Christ,

Pope Paul V

GALILEO

IN 1633, AN old man was called to stand trial in Rome. The man was celebrated Italian scientist Galileo Galilei. The charge? Heresy. The crime was his public support for Copernicus's views. Our courtroom reporter told the story.

IT WAS HARD to imagine that the frail 69-year-old man who stood before the court could pose a threat to anyone — let alone the power and might of the Christian Church. And yet according to the Pope, Galileo's beliefs concerning the workings of the universe challenge centuries of Christian teaching and are profoundly dangerous.

Galileo started off as a medical student but soon became more fascinated by heavenly bodies — the stars and the planets. In fact, it was he who first made the heavens more visible to countless astronomers. Before he did it, no one, as far as we know, ever thought of using a telescope for looking at the night sky.

THE MOMENT OF TRUTH

Using a telescope he had made himself, Galileo saw four moons orbiting the planet Jupiter. And therein lay his downfall. The existence of moons orbiting Jupiter convinced Galileo that the Earth was not the planet around which all other planets revolve.

He felt he had no option but to agree with Copernicus that the Sun, and not the Earth, is at the center of the universe, and it was this decision that triggered the bitter conflict with the Church, which eventually led to his arrest.

OVERSTEPPING THE MARK

Given that the Pope had already warned Galileo back in 1616 to abandon his support of Copernicus, many say it was an act of madness for him to publish his *Dialogue of the Two Great Systems of the World*. In this book, two men argue over the Copernican theory — one for, the other against. But anyone reading it is left in no doubt that the writer agrees with the person defending Copernicus.

Such a book was sure to anger the Church, and it was inevitable that its author would be charged with heresy — the crime

BROUGHT TO TRIAL

COURTROOM CRISIS: Galileo sits at the center of a crowd of clergymen, all eager to discover what the Church's decision will be.

The Bridgeman Art Library — 1632, Artist unknown

of opposing the Church.

Galileo's hands shook as the evidence, much of it from his own writing, piled up against him, yet he put up a spirited defense for his beliefs.

But in the end, hours of cross-examination left the elderly Galileo lacking enough strength to argue his case any further. Finally, he gave in to the prosecutor's request that he take back what he had said. He fell to his knees and reluctantly declared his opinion that the Earth moves around the Sun to be false.

All of Galileo's books are now banned. And the great man himself has been sentenced to a life of imprisonment within his own home.

As he was led away from the packed court-

room, some heard a last act of defiance when he muttered under his breath, "But the Earth does move!"

The Church may have silenced one old man for now, but given the strength of Galileo's evidence in favor of a Sun-centered universe, many people must be wondering how much longer it will be before the Church itself has to move its position on this issue. ☎

COPERNICAN THEORY REMAINED BANNED BY THE CHURCH UNTIL 1835, BUT AT LEAST A HUNDRED YEARS BEFORE THAT, MOST ASTRONOMERS HAD ACCEPTED THAT GALILEO HAD BEEN RIGHT TO SUPPORT IT. THE SCIENTISTS WHO CAME AFTER GALILEO

WANTED TO EXPLORE THE NATURAL WORLD AND ESTABLISH THE LAWS THAT GOVERN IT. THEY DEVISED WAYS OF PROVING THEIR DISCOVERIES SO THAT FOR THE FIRST TIME, PEOPLE BEGAN TO TAKE THE SUBJECT OF SCIENCE SERIOUSLY.

DEATH OF A SCIENTIST!

Illustrated by GINO D'ACHILLE

ALL WORK AND NO PLAY: Isaac Newton often became so absorbed in his work that he forgot to eat, wash, or even sleep for days on end.

WHEN SIR ISAAC NEWTON died in 1727, at the age of 84, The History News paid tribute to a great man by publishing the following article on his life, work, and extraordinary achievements.

IF HIS MOTHER had had her way, Isaac Newton would have been a farmer. But he was so hopeless at it that in 1664 she gave in to his wish to go to Cambridge University to study science.

Newton was a serious student who socialized little and worked late into the night, doggedly pursuing a subject until he had learned all he could about it. At first, he studied light and then conducted dozens of experiments to test his theories. These led him to make the amazing discovery that sunlight is made up of different colors—all the colors of the rainbow, in fact.

A MATTER OF SOME GRAVITY

In 1665, there was an outbreak of plague in Cambridge, and Newton went home to Lincolnshire. It is during this period that he is said to have thought up and written down his most important scientific theory.

While Newton was sitting under a tree, an apple fell from it and landed on his head. It is said that this helped him to realize that some kind of force must be pulling the apple toward the ground. He concluded that all objects give off a pulling force that attracts other objects to them, and the larger the object, the greater the force.

Newton called the force gravity, and his discovery explained such mysteries as why the Moon stays in orbit around the Earth—it is the force of gravity that holds it there.

In 1667, Newton went back to Cambridge. In 1669, at the age of 26, he was made the university's youngest-ever professor of mathematics. The next year, he invented a new kind of telescope, called a reflecting telescope, that could magnify objects to a greater extent than ever before.

Most people would have been content with these achievements, but Newton was relentless in his pursuit of knowledge. In 1687, he published his theories in a book called the *Principia*—now generally believed to be a masterpiece of scientific understanding. In this book he sets out his laws of motion—the ways in which objects will move in response to different external forces acting upon them.

CELEBRATED SCIENTIST

Elected President of the Royal Society in 1703, two years later Newton became the first scientist to be knighted by the King of England—a great honor, indeed!

Newton was not a man to suffer fools easily. He had a sharp tongue and he didn't hesitate to use it. But even those who disliked him could not deny that he was a brilliant scientist. His capacity to reason out a problem and back it up with evidence will set the standard for generations of scientists to come. 🌙

COMET MAKES A COMEBACK

EDMUND HALLEY predicted that the same comet which appeared in 1682 would return. But the world had to wait until 1758 to see if he was right.

WISE MAN: Halley predicts return of comet.

A GERMAN farmer has just reported seeing a comet above his home in Dresden. The timing of this sighting proves the theory held by the late astronomer Edmund Halley.

Back in 1682, Edmund Halley was so intrigued by the great comet of that year that he spent many years studying its path and comparing it with the records of previous comets.

He used some of Newton's Laws of Motion to calculate the movements of a comet that had previously been seen in 1607. He came to the conclusion that it must be the same one that had streaked across the sky in 1682.

He published his theories in 1705, stating boldly that the comet would make a reappearance in 1758.

He was right— it has just been confirmed. It will be visible for a few more months, then vanish for 76 years.

The History News has just learned that the Royal Society has proposed that the comet be named "Halley's Comet" in his honor. 🌙

"*To every action there is an equal and opposite reaction.*"

Isaac Newton's Third Law of Motion, 1687.

NEWTON'S LAW

OF ALL NEWTON'S Laws of Motion, the third law has had the greatest effect on the development of the space rocket. To non-scientists Newton's laws are not easy to understand, so we asked our space expert for a way of demonstrating how the third law works. And here's his answer . . .

ALL YOU NEED is a balloon. Blow it up, then let it go. The action of air rushing out from one end of the balloon causes it to move forward in the opposite direction from the expelled air. In other words, the balloon has an *equal and opposite reaction* to the air escaping.

To use a more practical example of this law in action, take the way that rockets work. Whether they're simple fireworks or space rockets, they all move in the same way. When fuel is burned inside the rocket, the fuel gives off gases which expand and rush out of the rocket.

The reaction of the rocket to the force of this downward rush of gas is to take off upward. 🌙

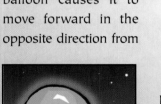

THE 1800s AND THE 1900s SAW SWEEPING ADVANCES IN KNOWLEDGE OF THE UNIVERSE. THE INVENTION OF PHOTOGRAPHY MEANT THAT ASTRONOMERS NO LONGER HAD TO RELY ON WORDS AND DRAWINGS TO RECORD WHAT THEY SAW.

AND THE DEVELOPMENT OF INCREASINGLY POWERFUL TELESCOPES MADE IT POSSIBLE FOR STARGAZERS TO PEER EVER DEEPER INTO SPACE. THE PLACES THAT EXCITED MOST CURIOSITY WERE OUR CLOSEST NEIGHBORS—MARS AND THE MOON.

IS THERE LIFE ON MARS?

Illustrated by IAN THOMPSON

WHEN, IN 1906, an American astronomer claimed he had proved the existence of intelligent life on Mars, it caused a sensation. At the time, *The History News* took a closer look at the facts behind the fiction surrounding the red planet.

FOR YEARS, astronomer Percival Lowell has been utterly fascinated by Mars. To keep an eye on the planet, he has had a superbly equipped observatory built in Arizona, where he has a telescope permanently trained on the red planet.

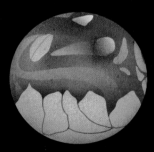

CHANNELS: Schiaparelli has the right view of Mars.

Among the many things he has noted are "canali," the lines that criss-cross the planet's surface. These were first spotted by Italian astronomer Giovanni Schiaparelli in 1877.

Lowell is convinced that the canals, as he calls them, are the creation of Martians—intelligent beings living there—and has written about them in his book *Mars and Its Canals*.

Having noted that the planet has very few clouds, he is convinced that there cannot be enough rain. Lowell writes that due to drought, the Martians have built the canals to carry water from ice caps at the planet's poles to provide for the dry areas.

Skeptics have pointed out that in order to be visible from Earth, the canals would have to be about 19 miles wide. But Lowell won't be shaken from his view. He is convinced that broad bands of irrigated land lie on either side of the massive canals.

Lowell writes that the Martians have built pumping stations and spaced them out at regular intervals along the canals to keep the water flowing.

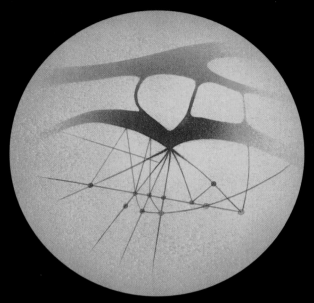

GOING TOO FAR: Lowell's canal idea isn't watertight.

Our science expert strongly believes that these theories are all products of Lowell's overactive imagination. Our expert has checked the dictionary definition of the Italian word "canali" and found that it does not mean canals at all, but channels—something that can be created by natural forces such as wind or movements in a planet's crust. It's his belief that the markings on Mars are the direct result of weather conditions and that the canal theory should be ditched. After all, when you look at it closely, it doesn't hold much water!

AN UPLIFTING EXPERIENCE

Illustrated by MIKE WHITE

SOMETIMES IT TAKES a leap of faith to make the unthinkable happen. In May 1926, our reporter had the good fortune to witness one committed scientist make such a leap. This is his account of that moment in space history.

ROBERT GODDARD first became fascinated by the possibility of space travel after reading the science fiction novels of Jules Verne and H.G. Wells. Since then, his scientific mind has led him to take their ideas a step further and to try to make fact out of fiction.

In 1919, Goddard, an American professor of physics, wrote a report in which he stated that the type of rocket necessary to reach the Moon would have to be a liquid-fueled one. Until now, rockets have run on gunpowder or solid fuel, so this notion was met with scorn and doubt by most newspaper reporters. They considered him a crackpot, and since then he has kept news of his work a secret. *The History News*, however, has always been sympathetic to his ideas, so he keeps us informed of his plans.

In view of his shyness and dislike of reporters, I felt honored when, in May 1926, he invited me to go to a field near his home in Massachusetts in order to witness the launch of the new rocket he had designed.

A cold May wind whipped across the field as 44-year-old Goddard, helped by four assistants and his loyal wife, brought a 9-foot-high metal contraption into place. After making the final checks, he lit the fuse of the rocket suspended in the metal frame.

UP, UP, AND AWAY

The downward rush of gas created by igniting a mixture of liquid oxygen and gasoline was enough to launch the rocket into the air. It took off at a steep angle and climbed some 40 feet before running out of fuel and falling to the ground, 185 feet away.

FLYING HIGH: Goddard demonstrates his rocket launcher.

The rocket's journey was short-lived, but the fact that it got higher and went faster than any other model was a brilliant breakthrough.

News of this success will confound Goddard's many critics. They will have to take him seriously from now on. Judging from this success, *The History News* is willing to bet that Goddard has cracked the secret of launching a powerful rocket—in time maybe even one that could achieve his dream and reach the Moon. 📞

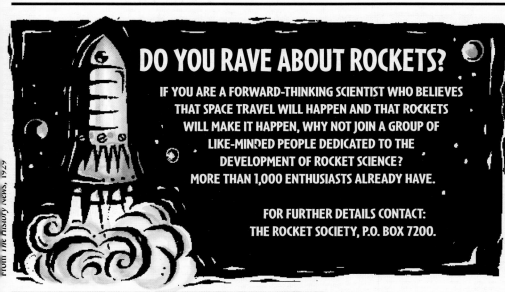

ROCKET MAN IN USA

Illustrated by ROGER GOODE

IN 1955, the man responsible for Germany's most deadly weapon during World War II became a US citizen. *The History News* investigated just why the Americans were so eager to have him on their side.

WHEN HE WAS JUST 18, Wernher von Braun joined the influential German Society for Space Travel—a group set up to encourage enthusiasts to pursue their dreams of space flight using rockets.

Then, after graduating with a degree in engineering, he was offered a job working on the German military's rocket program. The year was 1933. War, he says, didn't look likely at the time. He accepted the job because working for the military provided funding for rocket research, which was extremely expensive. He developed into a brilliant rocket scientist who used the principles set forth by the American rocket pioneer Robert Goddard. But unlike earlier rockets, von Braun's were used for

LETHAL WEAPON: A *V-2* travels faster than sound.

deadly *V-2* missiles during World War II. Some 13,000 of these huge flying bombs were launched from Germany and programmed to explode in British cities during the war. And as they could travel faster than the speed of sound, they were able to take their targets by surprise and cause the maximum devastation.

As WWII drew to a close and Germany was clearly on the verge of defeat, both America and the USSR had a common goal—to recruit rocket mastermind von Braun.

COLD WAR KICKS IN

During WWII, the two countries were allies, but in fact they were highly suspicious of each other. Each knew that the other was developing nuclear weapons, and each wanted von Braun and his team to build the rockets to carry them.

It was therefore a huge

relief to the Americans when, at the end of the war, the German rocket expert and his entire team surrendered to US troops. Over the past ten years, the mutual suspicion between the USA and the USSR has deepened into the hostility known as the Cold War. Armed conflict has been avoided so far, but there is nonetheless an intense sense of rivalry between the world's two superpowers.

Military authorities in both nations are pouring resources into rocket research—first, to ensure that they have the means to deliver nuclear weapons should the Cold War develop into a full-blown war and, equally importantly, to win the race into space.

Today, April 15, 1955, the world's foremost

rocket scientist, Wernher von Braun, held the Stars and Stripes flag in one hand and a Bible in the other, and swore his allegiance to become an American citizen.

Even though von Braun has been working in the United States for the past ten years, now that he is officially on their side, US scientists feel confident that it will be an American rocket that first leaves Earth's atmosphere and blasts into orbit.

Having said that, experts consulted by *The History News* say a Soviet rocket should not be ruled out of the running. After all, the race into space isn't over yet!

STAR MAN: Von Braun exhibits one of his rocket models.

TAKING IT IN STAGES

Illustrated by ROGER GOODE

THROUGHOUT the 1950s, scientists tried to invent a rocket powerful enough to counteract the pull of Earth's gravity. Toward the end of the decade, when they were close to a breakthrough, we ran this report on the rocket that might make the dream of space flight a reality . . .

✪ TACKLING GRAVITY
To date, no one has invented a rocket that is both light enough and fast enough to escape the Earth's atmosphere and reach outer space. The reason for this is gravity—the pull of Earth's gravity is so great that only a rocket large enough to carry a great deal of fuel can keep going forward and not fall back to Earth. Yet with so much fuel on board, the rocket would be too heavy to move fast enough. Now, rocket scientists say they have found an answer—it lies in multistage rockets.

✪ HOW IT WORKS
In a multistage rocket, each stage has its own fuel. Once the fuel has burned up, that stage then falls away and lightens the rocket's heavy load so that it is light enough to continue its journey.

✪ BLASTING AWAY
For takeoff, fuel and oxygen are released into the combustion chamber of stage one, where they ignite. The hot gases produced by the burning fuel escape through the exhaust nozzle at great speed. The force of this rush of gas leaving its exhaust pipe causes the rocket to shoot forward in the opposite direction and take off.

ROCKET ANATOMY

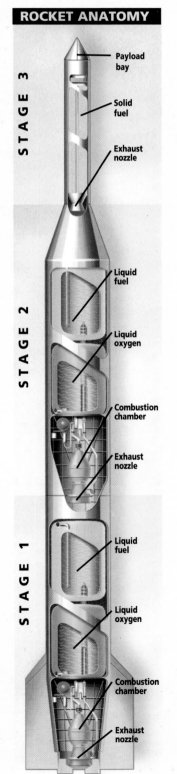

STAGE 3
- Payload bay
- Solid fuel
- Exhaust nozzle

STAGE 2
- Liquid fuel
- Liquid oxygen
- Combustion chamber
- Exhaust nozzle

STAGE 1
- Liquid fuel
- Liquid oxygen
- Combustion chamber
- Exhaust nozzle

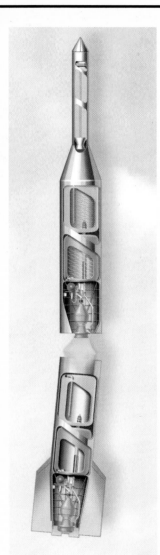

✪ TAKE A LOAD OFF
As soon as all the fuel in the first stage has burned up, it separates from the rocket and falls away. The rocket does not lose any speed because as the first stage detaches the second ignites, giving the rocket enough thrust to continue its journey.

✪ FINAL STAGES
Once the fuel tanks in the second stage are empty, it too falls away, and the third stage takes over.

By this time, the rocket is approaching outer space—at about 13,000 miles per hour. This is the speed that a rocket must reach in order to counteract the force of the Earth's strong gravitational pull and go into orbit.

✪ ORBITING FREE
Once in orbit, the rocket is ready to free its cargo—the all-important payload. Its controls will have been pre-set so that the cone at its tip splits apart and falls away, releasing the payload inside. The first kind of payload that scientists try to send into space will be a radio satellite that is programmed to send signals back to Earth so that it can be located.

✪ WHAT NEXT?
Building a rocket like this is complicated, but we feel certain that one day soon scientists will have the technology to do it. In fact, *The History News* predicts that a new age is about to dawn—in which space flight will be an everyday event. ⟲

SATELLITE TO THE STARS

Illustrated by PETER VISSCHER

IN 1957, the USSR hit the world's headlines with the momentous news that it had finally sent a satellite into orbit. *The History News* was quick to report on the shock waves that followed.

YESTERDAY, October 4, 1957, will go down in history as the day the USSR took the world by surprise and put a man-made satellite—*Sputnik 1*—into space.

Space experts in the USA are still reeling from the news. They had heard about Moscow radio broadcasts announcing a launch. They had even been given details of the radio frequency on which the "beep-beep" of the satellite's signal would be heard. Yet the Americans had been sure that the Soviets were deliberately trying to mislead them.

Well, all those cynics will have to eat their words now — the Soviets weren't bluffing!

Sputnik (Russian for "traveler") was launched at Baikonour Cosmodrome in Soviet Central Asia. Eyewitnesses described seeing flames shoot out from the rocket's engines. Seconds later a roar like thunder echoed around the site, and the rocket was shrouded in clouds of vapor. Then it rose from the launch pad and, as it soared, a raging flame lit up the night sky.

The men who had been working on the project embraced one another, clearly overjoyed that the mission had gotten off to a flying start.

BREAKING FREE: The cone of the launch rocket splits open, releasing *Sputnik 1* into orbit.

Once in orbit, the rocket released its tiny payload, and now *Sputnik*—just 23 inches in diameter—is orbiting the Earth at a speed of 17,600 miles per hour and at a height of 582 miles above the ground. And it is sending signals back to Earth so that its position can be located and every detail of its journey can be monitored.

Sputnik is expected to remain in orbit for up to 90 days before falling back to Earth.

CRASH AND BURN

By the end of 90 days in orbit, *Sputnik* will be traveling at such a high speed through the Earth's atmosphere that the air surrounding it will heat up and the satellite will be burned to a frazzle.

It is difficult to overestimate what a historic event this is, and what a coup it is for the USSR in their race to be first into space. They have proved the excellence of their space technology and overtaken their rival—the USA. Today, the USSR must be the proudest nation on the planet.

SPACEMAN'S BEST FRIEND

ONE MONTH after the launch of *Sputnik 1*, the USSR scored another space first, and the day when rockets would carry human passengers came a step closer.

TONIGHT, there's a brand new star in the sky—a small Soviet dog named Laika.

Earlier today, the brown-and-white dog was locked in a special padded and pressurized compartment inside *Sputnik 2* and sent into orbit. Laika has become the first creature to travel in space—the first canine cosmonaut!

Sadly, this exciting mission has a built-in tragedy. After ten days in space, Laika will have used up her air supply. She will lose consciousness and die in her sleep.

Sputnik 2 will then complete its five-month voyage before burning up when it re-enters the Earth's atmosphere.

IT'S A DOG'S LIFE

Animal lovers are protesting about what they consider to be an act of cruelty. But scientists argue that through electrodes attached to her, Laika is providing them with vital information about the way an animal's body reacts to being in space.

Most important, scientists will know more about how a human might react to space flight. ☾

ON A MISSION: Spacehound gets set for flight.

Sovfoto/Eastfoto

FIRST US FLIGHT FAILS

Illustrated by PETER VISSCHER

DOWN IN FLAMES: The US *Vanguard* project is just hot air.

DESPERATE TO GET its own satellite into orbit, America set the launch date of its *Vanguard* rocket for December 1957. Our reporter was at the scene.

FOR TWO DAYS I'd been kicking my heels at Cape Canaveral in Florida, waiting for the much-talked-about launch of the first US satellite into orbit. There had been a long series of delays. So it was a relief to be assured by officials that it would definitely happen before midday today, December 6.

The countdown went smoothly. But seconds after the engines were fired, the three-stage *Vanguard* rocket erupted in a ball of flames and toppled over.

Officials looked on, horror-struck, as the rocket's nose cone was thrown clear of the inferno and the little satellite rolled across the launch pad, bleeping pathetically.

In the light of this disaster, the US Navy-designed *Vanguard* rocket will doubtless be ditched in favor of a rival model currently being developed by the brilliant Wernher von Braun. Even so, having witnessed today's flop, I can't help wondering whether the US space program will ever get off the ground! ☾

MAN IN SPACE!

■ Illustrated by CHRISTIAN HOOK ■

THE USSR'S RUN of space-success stories reached an all-time high on April 12, 1961, when it sent a man into orbit. *The History News* talked to the first-ever space hero, Yuri Gagarin.

❓ How did you come to be the first cosmonaut?

Back in 1959, I was a pilot in the Soviet Air Force. I heard the authorities were looking for men to train as cosmonauts.

Dozens of us applied, but not many passed the grueling tests and were accepted. I was thrilled to be among the chosen few, but I wasn't able to share my excitement with anyone else — we were all sworn to secrecy. I couldn't even tell my wife.

The training was really tough, but each one of us was determined that the Soviet Union should get a man into space before the USA. We trained for six months — getting in shape, going through the launch and landing procedures again and again.

It wasn't until a few days before the launch that my commander told me that I had been chosen from among my comrades to be the first cosmonaut. I thought I would burst with pride!

❓ Can you describe the moment of takeoff?

My space capsule — *Vostok 1* — was at the top of an *A1* ballistic missile

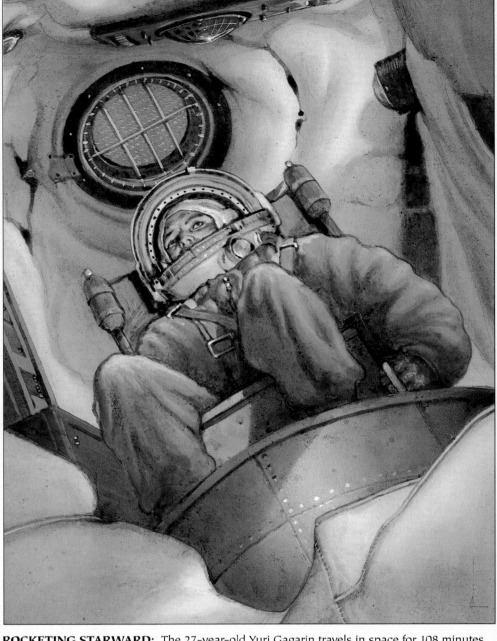

ROCKETING STARWARD: The 27-year-old Yuri Gagarin travels in space for 108 minutes.

rocket. The rocket had been specially adapted from a weapon of war to a launch vehicle for my flight. In the elevator up to the capsule I didn't feel at all nervous, just excited about the great adventure that lay ahead of me.

I was helped into the capsule and strapped into my seat. The force of the thrust when the engines lit was incredibly powerful. As the rocket surged upward I could hear each of the stages

drop away. Then all that was left was me, traveling through space in my capsule.

❓ What was it like being in space?

I felt like a stranger in my own body. If I hadn't been strapped in, I'd have floated off my seat.

As I lay there I saw a pencil and notebook drift in front of me. Through

the porthole the sky was black, yet the Earth was startlingly bright on the sunlit side. I couldn't take my eyes off it.

The time went by in a flash, even though I had little to do — *Vostok 1* was designed to fly on automatic pilot, directed by ground control.

I was rocketing through space at 5 miles per second, and after 89 minutes, I had circled the Earth twice and it was time to come down.

How did that go?

On returning to Earth's atmosphere, re-entry burn shrouded my capsule in enormous flames.

At 4.5 miles above ground, the escape hatch blew open and I was ejected, still strapped to my seat. I could see the seat's parachute billowing above me as I fell to 2.5 miles.

Then I separated from the seat and used my own parachute, which was attached to my back, for the rest of the descent.

On my return to Earth, I was given a hero's welcome, and learned that while I was in orbit, I had been promoted from lieutenant to major. The day after I landed, I was awarded the "Order of Lenin" for services to my country. I never dreamed I would ever receive such an honor.

You're not just a hero in the Soviet Union!

I know. I hear there are souvenirs with my face on them for sale all over the world. It's as if people of all nations want to celebrate the fact that the day of manned space flight has arrived.

Has the space flight changed your life?

Of course. My life has changed dramatically. I'm now invited to space conferences all over the world. I miss flying, but I'm proud to represent my country as a kind of ambassador, promoting Soviet space technology everywhere I go.

My flight was a great triumph for the USSR, but I tell you, when you've looked down on the world from so far above it, you don't see the boundaries separating one nation from another, you just see one uniquely beautiful planet, floating in a black sky. 🄲

HOMETOWN HERO: Gagarin becomes a celebrity overnight.

PRESIDENT AIMS FOR THE MOON

FROM THE TOP: Kennedy pledges US lunar landing.

BEGINNING IN MAY 1961, the US space program had a powerful new driving force behind it — the American president himself — as this report revealed . . .

TODAY, PRESIDENT John F. Kennedy astonished the US Congress, and the world, in a speech that brought scores of cheering politicians to their feet as he pledged to put an American on the Moon.

For almost ten years now, space has been the battleground of the Cold War between the USA and the USSR, with each nation keeping its plans a closely guarded secret.

Today, the president has changed all that by publicly declaring, "I believe the nation should commit itself to achieving the goal, before the decade is out, of landing a man on the Moon and returning him safely to Earth." With his voice soaring above the applause, he declared that getting to the Moon before the Soviets is a challenge that America intends to meet.

PROMISING THE MOON

Kennedy has thrown down the gauntlet to the Soviets. And now one thing is certain — the race to the Moon is in high gear. 🄲

AMERICA OVERTAKES

THROUGHOUT THE 1960s, space technology raced ahead. At first the USSR hogged the headlines, but as the decade progressed, the US space program came into its own — as these articles reveal.

SOVIET STEPS OUT

HANGING AROUND: Leonov floats in space.

NEWS HAS just reached us of another stunning Soviet space triumph — a cosmonaut has just floated in outer space.

SOVIETS HAVE been walking on air since Aleksei Leonov made a space record yesterday, March 18, 1965, by taking a stroll. He squeezed through the escape hatch of his spacecraft, *Voskhod 2*, while it was in orbit, and became the first man to step out into space.

Thanks to a television camera mounted in the capsule, millions watched the USSR's latest space pioneer twirling around on a safety cord attached to the capsule.

With an oxygen tank strapped to his back so he could breathe, Leonov enjoyed a 12-minute float in space before returning to the hatch. But to his horror, his spacesuit had ballooned, and he couldn't fit back inside.

A tense 8 minutes went by while he released some of the air pressure in the suit and let it shrink enough for him to squeeze to safety, luckily none the worse for his ordeal. ☪

FIRST LADY OF SPACE

THE USSR had another surprise in store for the world today when it sent the first woman into space . . .

THE WORLD has a new heroine — Soviet-born Valentina Tereshkova has realized her ambition to become the first woman in space.

Inspired by Gagarin's amazing feat, Valentina Tereshkova, a factory worker with parachuting experience, wrote to Soviet President Kruschev and asked to follow in her hero's footsteps. She was allowed to train as a cosmonaut, and on June 16, 1963, her wish to be sent on a mission into space was granted.

After it had orbited the Earth 48 times, her spacecraft landed safely back on Soviet soil. She emerged triumphant, having been in orbit for three days. ☪

FLYING HIGH: A dream comes true for Tereshkova.

TRAGEDY STRIKES

THE USSR'S *Soyuz* test flight in preparation for landing on the Moon has ended in tragedy here on Earth, as our reporter explains.

THE USSR HAS suffered a blow with the news that *Soyuz 1* crashed to Earth yesterday, April 24, 1967, killing its cosmonaut, Vladimir Komarov. The launch had gone well although there were a few problems during the flight. Then on the craft's re-entry from orbit, the parachute lines of Komarov's capsule became tangled and caused the fatal accident on landing. The tragedy casts doubt on the future of the entire *Soyuz* program. ☪

USSR IN SPACE RACE

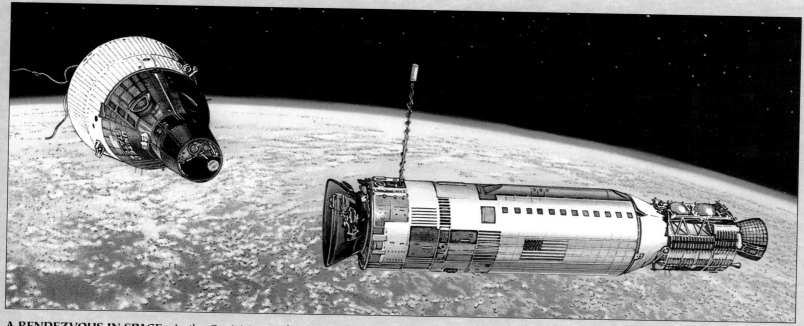

A RENDEZVOUS IN SPACE: As the *Gemini 8* capsule nears the *Agena* rocket, both are right on target for their historic docking.

REACHING FOR THE MOON

Illustrated by PETER VISSCHER

SO FAR, THE RACE to reach the Moon has been dominated by one Soviet success story after another, but if you thought it was all over for the Americans, think again. They have just scored some advances of their own . . .

DURING the last seven years, NASA has devoted its energies to two space programs—Gemini and Apollo—both aiming for a voyage to the Moon.

The Gemini series has been a spectacular success. Its many triumphs have included America's first multi-crewed flight, its first space walk, and, most important of all, the moment in 1966 when Neil Armstrong and David Scott linked up, or docked, *Gemini 8* to an *Agena* rocket.

This significant event means that scientists at NASA at last know for certain that if a manned spacecraft is landed on the Moon as it is hoped will happen by the end of the 1960s, and can be successfully relaunched from there, the astronauts aboard will be able to dock with an orbiting spacecraft and be carried back to Earth.

The very first of the many Apollo missions, however, got off to a bad start in January 1967, when three astronauts died in a fire during training.

But on December 21, 1968, NASA had a breakthrough when the crew of *Apollo 8* made a safe launch. They went into orbit around the Moon on December 24.

The crew achieved a fistful of firsts—they were the first men to venture farther than 840 miles into space, the first to view the entire Earth from space, and the first to orbit the Moon and see its far side.

Apollo 8's pictures of Earth and of the Moon's lifeless surface were broadcast on television for the whole world to see. This truly historic transmission reminded us how precious our life-sustaining planet is.

After 10 orbits over a period of 16 hours, James Lovell fired the spacecraft's main engine, setting the capsule on course for a Pacific Ocean splashdown.

The History News is reliably informed that US space experts at NASA are now confident that the day when an American walks on the Moon may be just about to dawn.

A GIANT LEAP FOR MANKIND

O N JULY 20, 1969, Neil Armstrong climbed down the ladder of the lunar module *Eagle* and became the first human being to stand on the surface of the Moon. *The History News* gave a glowing report of this monumental milestone in the history of space exploration . . .

MOON LANDING: Aldrin takes his first step on the Moon

ONE-FIFTH of the entire population of the world watched TV in wonder as American astronaut Neil Armstrong stepped onto the surface of the Moon.

"That's one small step for man, one giant leap for mankind," his voice crackled on the airwaves and echoed around mission control at Houston,

Texas, 238,000 miles away.

A few seconds later, Armstrong was joined on the surface by Edwin "Buzz" Aldrin. The third member of the crew, Michael Collins, was still in orbit around the Moon. He had remained in *Apollo 11*'s command module, *Columbia*.

The three men left

Earth in *Apollo 11* on July 16, thrust into space by the awesomely powerful *Saturn 5* rocket.

It was around noon four days later when Armstrong and Aldrin first crawled into the

Apollo 11's lunar module, the *Eagle*, to begin the descent procedure. Half an hour later, Collins pressed the button that released the *Eagle* from *Columbia* and sent it on its way down to the Moon. Minutes later Armstrong told mission control, "The *Eagle* has landed." The answer

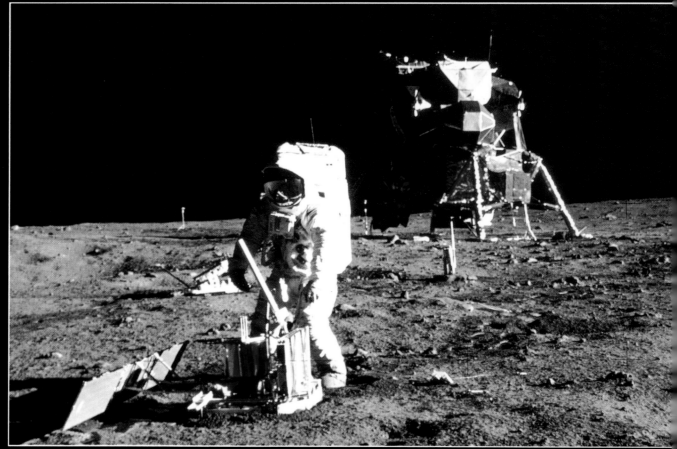

HISTORY IN THE MAKING: *Apollo 11* blasts off from Earth (left), and Buzz Aldrin collects Moon rocks, photographed in front of the lunar module (above).

from mission control was a huge sigh of relief, and a message went back to the Moon saying, "We're breathing again. Thanks a lot."

Armstrong's next task was to pull a cord on the *Eagle* and lower a live television camera. A few minutes later, 600 million people watched him take his historic step.

In years to come, people are bound to ask each other, "Where were you the day that Neil Armstrong walked on the Moon?" All who watched it happen knew it was one of those memorable moments—the fulfillment of an age-old dream.

WALKING ON THE MOON

Armstrong and Aldrin explored the area of the Moon where they had landed. They proudly erected a US flag that had a special wire frame to hold it up since there is

no wind to carry it. Then they collected samples of the rocks that litter the Moon's landscape to take back for laboratory analysis on Earth.

Using a hand-held still camera, Armstrong took reels and reels of film, knowing that the curiosity of the entire world would have been aroused by this mission and the more information they could bring back, the better.

COMING BACK DOWN TO EARTH

Having completed their tasks, the pair returned to *Eagle*, ignited the engine, and headed for their rendezvous in space with *Columbia*. Once again, all plans went like clockwork, and *Eagle* docked safely with *Columbia*.

The *Apollo 11* spacecraft splashed down in the Pacific Ocean four days later. What a warm welcome awaited the men from the Moon when they came back down to Earth!

OVER THE MOON: *Apollo 11* astronauts in celebratory parade.

MOTORING MOON-STYLE

ROVER STAR RATING	
Looks	★
Speed	★
Comfort	★
Suitability	★★★★★

NASA

MOON-WORTHY: It takes a special kind of buggy to go for a drive on the Moon.

THE ASTRONAUTS of *Apollo 15* who landed on the Moon in August 1971 didn't have to rely on their legs to get around—they took a car. *The History News* gave the Lunar Rover the once-over.

DESIGNED BY a US aircraft engineering company, the Lunar Roving Vehicle, or LRV, cost millions of dollars to build for a single drive on the Moon.

Its special features include a collapsible chassis, so it can be stowed neatly on the outside of the lunar module during flight. Then on landing, all the astronauts have to do is pull a cord and—

presto—the buggy drops down and unfolds automatically.

Batteries positioned above each of the four wheels give the LRV enough power to travel 55 miles—farther than the astronauts could go on foot.

SPECIALLY MADE FOR THE MOON

Easily controlled by a single hand lever, and

with a Moon weight of just 77 pounds, the buggy is ideally suited to the Moon's low gravity conditions.

There's plenty of storage space to transport samples of Moon rock, and the camera attached to the buggy's controls means that there's a complete photographic record of the journey.

The Lunar Rover does have one major flaw though—it can't be used again. On completion of the mission, the buggy will be left behind, making it the most expensive abandoned car in history!

SHAPING UP FOR SPACE

Illustrated by WILLIE RYAN

THROUGHOUT THE LATE 1960s and early 1970s, every kid in America was dreaming of walking on the Moon. *The History News* decided it was time to talk to one of the US pilots selected to follow in Neil Armstrong's footsteps. Here's his inside story on what it really took to become an astronaut back then.

☑ FITTING THE BILL

I had the basics required by NASA to get into the space program. I'm in shape, intelligent, less than 6 feet tall, and I weigh under 180 pounds. The medical test was rigorous, but I passed. I've been a jet pilot for five years, so flying is no problem. But training to be an astronaut is no easy ride!

☑ UNDER PRESSURE

The air pressure inside a space capsule is kept the same as it is on Earth. If an accident makes this pressure level drop, you can get decompression sickness, which causes muscle pain and breathing difficulties. So as part of my training, I had to be tested to see how little pressure I could take. I was locked inside a special chamber where the air pressure was steadily reduced while doctors assessed how well my body stood up to it.

☑ GOING FOR A SPIN

G-force—the enormous pressure of gravity that astronauts experience when their spacecraft both accelerates for lift-off and decelerates for re-entry—is strong enough to send even a rhinoceros reeling!

To give me a taste of what G-force feels like, I was strapped into a seat inside a centrifuge machine and spun around and around at high speed. I felt as if my brain was bursting!

☑ GETTING THE DRIFT

Apparently, moving about in space feels like floating in water, so dressed in a space suit, I was dropped into a huge pool called a neutral buoyancy tank. I had to move around and perform tasks that are similar to the kind of work I'd have to do in space, such as checking the safety of the craft. It was hard work trying to move in water with all that gear on!

☑ FLOATING AROUND

Once you get far away from the powerful pull of Earth's gravity, your body starts to become weightless. To get used to this sensation, I was flown up to a great height inside a plane, which then plummeted downward so rapidly I found myself in complete free fall, just floating above the cabin floor.

☑ A ROUGH RIDE

After Neil Armstrong had completed the very first successful space docking in 1966, a vital piece of his spacecraft's steering apparatus malfunctioned, and the craft went into a hair-raising spin. It was brought under control, but in case it happens again, today's astronauts have to be prepared. So I was strapped into a multi-axis wheel and spun first in one direction, then another, head over heels, around and around. It's a good thing I have a strong stomach—some of the other guys felt really sick after this one!

☑ MAKING A SPLASH

All US missions end with a splashdown in the ocean. Being put into a space capsule simulator aboard a plane, then dropped from a point above the Atlantic Ocean gave me a rough idea of what it feels like to come back down to Earth after a space flight.

☑ A GOOD RESULT

I made the grade! After three years of training, I'm an astronaut. Of course, that doesn't mean I'll be selected for a space flight, but at least I have a good chance! ☜

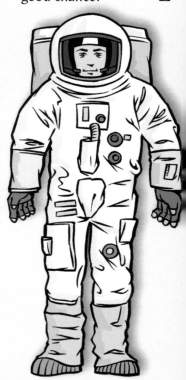

NASA

FLYING INTO SPACE: The amazing US shuttle looks a lot like an ordinary airplane.

THE SHUTTLE TAKES OFF!

EVEN BEFORE they had landed a man on the Moon, US scientists were planning the next stage in the space program—a spacecraft that could be reused. In 1981, NASA invited *The History News* to attend a very special launch . . .

NINE YEARS have passed since President Richard Nixon approved plans to spend $5.1 billion on developing a reusable spaceship. The plan had had many setbacks, but on April 12, 1981, at 7:00 A.M., a winged spacecraft, looking a lot like an ordinary airplane, was rocketed into space on the back of a massive fuel tank and two rocket boosters.

Two minutes later, the boosters burned out and fell to Earth, where they were recovered to be used on future shuttle missions.

Eight minutes into the flight, the now empty fuel tank fell away and the spacecraft *Columbia* went into orbit.

Columbia orbited Earth 36 times during the 54-hour mission. Commander John Young reported throughout the flight that everything was going smoothly. Then came a nerve-racking silence when radio control was lost as the shuttle burst back into the Earth's atmosphere at 17,360 miles per hour, generating a heat so intense the spacecraft would be white-hot.

MAKE OR BREAK TIME

The special tiles glued to the spacecraft protected it from the intense heat. And with the world's eyes watching, *Columbia* glided into view right on schedule and made a perfect landing.

It is hoped that the new spacecraft will be used to carry people and freight back and forth between Earth and NASA's next great plan—a permanent station in space. Now, the success of the shuttle has brought that goal one step closer to reality.

Editor's Note: Although *Columbia* was a great success, the US shuttle program was marked by tragedy in 1986 when *Challenger* exploded shortly after launching. All seven crew members, including schoolteacher Christa McAuliffe, died in the terrible accident.

SHUTTLING INTO SPACE

LAUNCH
The shuttle's main engines ignite, then build up to full power, and when the solid-fueled rockets ignite, we have liftoff.

TWO MINUTES LATER
Solid-fueled boosters burn out and separate from the shuttle.

EIGHT MINUTES GO BY
The main engines continue to fire until the shuttle reaches the outer edge of Earth's atmosphere. The empty external tank separates, and the craft enters orbit.

LANDING
Heat-resistant tiles protect the shuttle as it re-enters Earth's atmosphere. Its wings help the shuttle decelerate at a steady pace, and then the crew prepares the craft for landing—as it would a plane.

LIFE IN SPACE

During the 1970s, both the USA and the USSR were launching their own manned stations in space—for military, scientific, and research purposes. As in the past, the Soviets were ahead of the game.

✪ APRIL 1971

The first space station, *Salyut 1*, 47 feet long and 13 feet across, is launched by the USSR.

✪ JUNE 1971

Cosmonauts from the USSR spend three weeks in *Salyut 1*. On their return journey to Earth, the air in their spacecraft, *Soyuz 11*, is released into space when a valve opens by accident, killing all three of them.

✪ OCTOBER 1971

Salyut 1 burns up on re-entering Earth's atmosphere.

✪ MAY 1973

USA launches *Skylab*. It is 118 feet long and 21 feet across. It stays in orbit for 75 months, but is occupied for only six.

✪ JULY 1975

Two cosmonauts set the space endurance record by staying on *Salyut 4* for 63 days.

✪ FEBRUARY 1986

USSR launches *Mir*, a modular space station that can house up to six cosmonauts.

IN 1986, THE Soviets put their *Mir* space station into orbit, and there were reports of countless astronauts going back and forth. *The History News* brings you the inside story of what it was like to actually live in space . . .

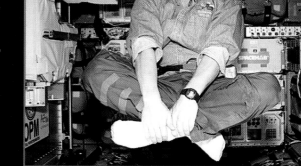

FAR OUT: An astronaut relaxes by floating in space.

ALL IN A DAY'S WORK

While they are on board the space laboratory, astronauts have various tasks to carry out. The majority of their time is spent doing routine maintenance work on the equipment inside the spacecraft, or checking the state of repair of the outside of the craft.

Often, astronauts will work on experiments in the laboratory. Many of these are aimed at finding out how the human body reacts to being in space for an extended period of time.

Other visitors may just be on board for a short time—for a specific mission, such as carrying out special observations of the Earth.

---✪---

TIME FOR PLAY

It's not all work and no play on board a space station—astronauts need their leisure time. Many of them relax by reading, playing cards, or enjoying the sensation of weightlessness that you get in space by floating around and practicing space-style somersaults.

Some astronauts take aboard collapsible guitars and other small musical instruments, and all of them spend a lot of time staring out of the window, admiring the Earth far below.

---✪---

WHAT TO WEAR

Astronauts only wear space suits when they are working on the outside of the space station, and when they are traveling. Most of the men and women working on *Mir* wear loose, comfortable clothing, such as overalls. Dirty clothes are stored and then brought home.

---✪---

FOOD FOR THOUGHT

Astronauts need about 2,900 calories a day and require a balanced diet. Fresh food supplies are limited due to lack of room to store them. So a lot of the food on board a space station is dehydrated, and water has to be injected into it to make it edible. A typical meal might consist of sweet and sour beef with rice, and fruit and nuts for dessert.

As there is no "down" in zero gravity, it is impossible to drink liquid from an open cup—astronauts have to use a covered cup and straw.

---✪---

KEEPING CLEAN

In zero gravity, it's difficult to control the direction of the water coming out of the shower-head. And the astronauts' feet have to be strapped to the floor of the shower unit inside rubber slippers so that their bodies don't float away.

Mir also has specially designed toilets. They're fitted with seatbelts to prevent the astronauts from drifting off. And

HARD AT WORK: Equipment needs constant monitoring.

since there is no gravity to pull the waste down into the toilet bowl, this is done by an air-suction device. Either the waste is stored and returned to Earth at the end of the mission, or else it is ejected into space.

STAYING HEALTHY

The down side of living in zero gravity is that the body responds in peculiar ways to this complete change. For a start, with no gravity to pull body fluids down, they all float upward, making the body appear fat and bloated. In order to counteract this, astronauts have to wear belts strapped around the top of each leg. The effect of zero gravity on muscles is to weaken them. To prevent any serious damage to their bodies, astronauts have to spend time on an exercise bike or rowing machine.

NODDING OFF

Astronauts need their sleep like the rest of us, but it's difficult to drop off when the space station is bathed in sunlight for half of its 92-minute orbit. So most of them use a mask.

Their sleeping bags are strapped to the wall of the spacecraft, and most astronauts sleep standing up inside them. They find it's more comfortable than lying strapped to the floor.

THE FUTURE

As astronauts spend longer periods in space, carrying out complex experiments, the question of their comfort becomes ever more important to those who design space stations.

In the past, it was the mission itself that was most important. Take the first man in space, for

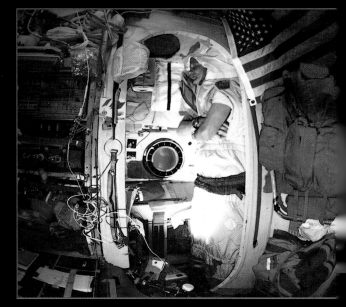

STRAPPED IN: Most astronauts sleep in an upright positio[n]

example—no one paid much attention to the Yuri Gagarin's comfort during his flight. But today the astronauts' welfare is treated with a lot more consideration The future success o space stations depends on it.

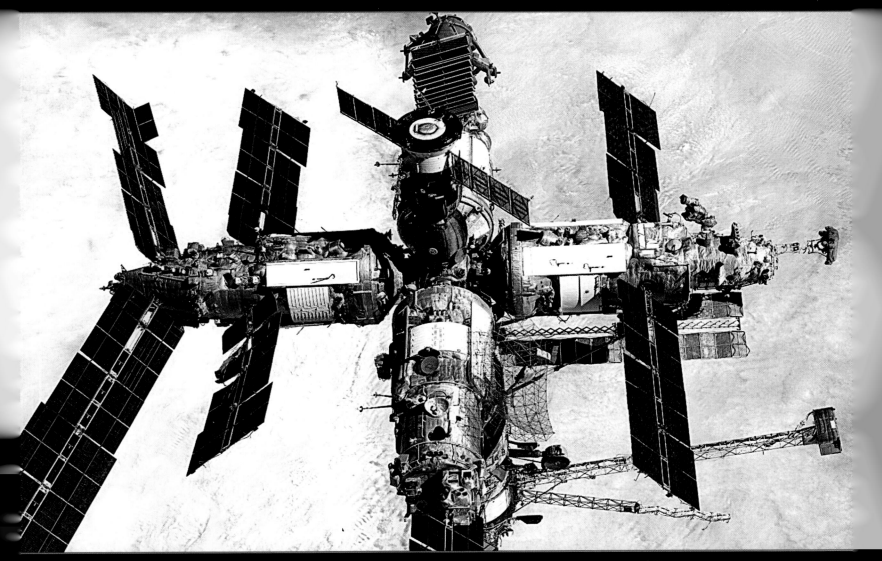

THE ORBITING OFFICE: Since its launch, new space labs and docking ports have been added to improve *Mir*'s capability.

PROBING THE LIMITS

BACK IN 1977, NASA launched twin space probes, *Voyagers 1* and *2*, on an ambitious mission to reach the outer planets. Today, August 25, 1989, news just in from *Voyager 2* has amazed even the most optimistic of NASA's space scientists . . .

JUBILANT NASA scientists are poring over the most sensational images of distant planets ever to be relayed back to Earth.

The *Voyager 1* and *Voyager 2* space probes were originally launched to go to areas of the solar system too far away to be reached by manned spacecraft.

Voyager 1 was launched in September 1977, a few days after *Voyager 2*. And in 1981, having sent back crystal-clear photographs and new data about the planets Jupiter and Saturn, *Voyager 1* left the solar system. Unfortunately, at this point, its signals became too weak to be picked up on Earth.

MANY A MOON

Meanwhile, *Voyager 2* stayed on course to make two more discoveries. Three years ago, it closed in on Uranus and detected ten previously unknown moons orbiting the cloud covered planet. Then it went on to Neptune.

Until now, scientists thought that Neptune had two moons. But thanks to *Voyager 2*, we now know that it has eight, and the largest of these, Triton, is the coldest known place in the solar system.

Photographs that have just come in from *Voyager 2* reveal details of a frozen wasteland with geysers that spurt out dust and nitrogen gas.

Voyager 2 has also revealed that Neptune is lashed by fierce winds. And an enormous blue spot seen in the planet's atmosphere is really a violent storm, big enough to engulf the Earth.

But even more exciting than these images of our solar system is the prospect of learning what lies beyond it. Yes, mind-boggling though it may sound, scientists believe that they will be able to keep track of *Voyager 2* until the year 2030. At that stage, it will be 5,209,000,000 miles away from Earth.

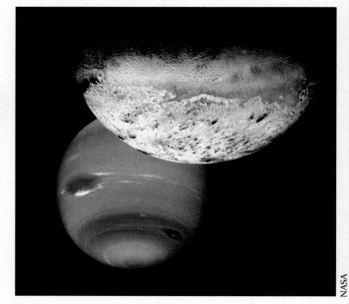

SNAP HAPPY: *Voyager 2* pictures of Neptune and Triton.

FACTS STRANGER THAN FICTION

In anticipation of this, scientists have equipped *Voyager 2* with messages for any alien life forms it might encounter.

A disc attached to the probe contains a CD on which greetings in 60 different languages have been recorded. It seems strange, but who knows what or who might respond to its signals when *Voyager 2* leaves our solar system? Whatever it is, you can be sure you'll read about it first in *The History News*.

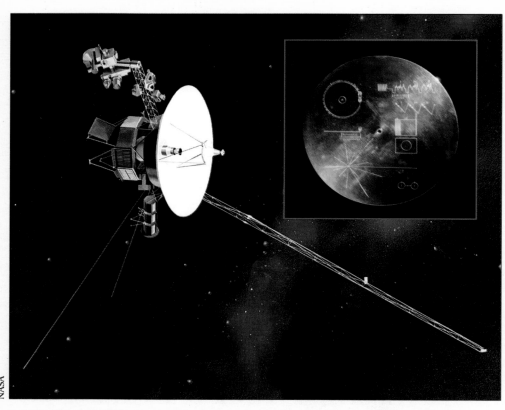

THE LONE RANGER: *Voyager 2* is equipped with antennae for sending signals back to Earth, a camera for recording images, even a special CD for aliens to decode (inset picture).

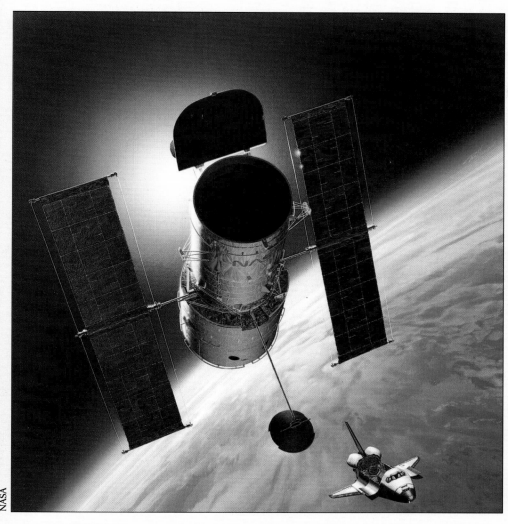

PERFECT VISION: The space shuttle leaves *Hubble* having repaired its all-important lens.

HUBBLE IN TROUBLE!

THE *HUBBLE TELESCOPE*, which was put into orbit in 1990 to peer into space from a position high above the Earth's atmosphere, was very nearly an expensive flop, as this report from 1993 reveals.

IT WAS BACK in the 1960s that NASA first began to look at the practicality of sending a huge telescope into orbit around Earth.

Even with the powerful telescopes scientists use today, they cannot see well enough through the Earth's hazy atmosphere to get a true picture. To get a good picture of the workings of our solar system, astronomers decided they needed an orbital telescope. So NASA came up with the world's biggest and best-ever telescope — the *Hubble*.

Named after American astronomer Edwin Powell Hubble, the *Hubble Space Telescope*, or *HST*, was built with the aid of many European countries. It has huge winglike solar panels to power its various complex systems and instruments.

Inside the telescope, there are two cameras, and two spectrometers — devices that split up light from a star or galaxy and examine it in the most minute detail — as well as a photometer, which measures the brightness of what is seen.

A SHORT-SIGHTED TELESCOPE

Hubble was launched with great expectations in April 1990 and was intended to stay in orbit for 15 years. Yet within a mere 8 months, NASA scientists reluctantly admitted that they had detected a flaw — the *Hubble Space Telescope* couldn't focus properly. Astronomers' hopes of having a clear eye fixed on the universe were dashed.

There was just one chance — it might be possible to repair the faulty lens. At a cost of 1.5 billion dollars, the replacement equipment was made, and astronauts on board the space shuttle *Endeavor* flew it out to *Hubble* to do the repairs.

New pictures just in prove that the operation was a success! *Hubble*'s fuzzy vision is a thing of the past. And the telescope has already made up for lost time by producing fantastic shots of space miracles — from the birth of galaxies to the death of stars.

Undaunted by their initial setback, NASA astronomers predict that in the not too distant future, scientists will one day be able to work out the exact size and age of the universe just by studying *Hubble*'s observations. Now that would be amazing!

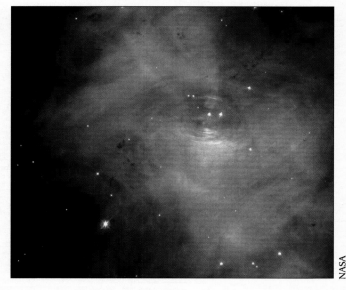

A STAR IS BORN: *Hubble* picks up images of new stars in the Crab Nebula — a vast cloud of gas and dust in deep space.

NEW HORIZONS OPEN UP

WELCOME TO MARS: While *Sojourner* heads off on its mission to check out Martian rocks, the *Pathfinder* lander beams this photo back to Earth.

IMAGINE being able to drive a remote-controlled car over the surface of another planet. Well, in July 1997, that's exactly what NASA scientists on Earth were doing on Mars—as this report on the *Pathfinder* mission reveals.

MARS HAS long held a deep fascination for scientists. For one thing, it's the planet that is our nearest neighbor, but more important, it's also the planet that experts believe we could one day live on.

With the exception of the US Mariner and Viking programs of the 1960s and 1970s, most missions to Mars have ended in failure. As a result, Mars has come to be regarded as the "unlucky planet."

Now the *Pathfinder* mission to Mars has surprised everyone by turning out to be a stunning success.

Pathfinder is the first of NASA's Discovery series of missions. The aim of these missions will be to explore space quickly and cheaply.

After a seven-month journey from Earth, *Pathfinder* entered the Martian atmosphere on July 4, 1997. Its descent was slowed down by a parachute, then small retro-rockets. Just before the spacecraft would have hit the Martian surface, giant airbags inflated and bounced *Pathfinder* to a safe landing. This was the first time this cost-effective system of landing a spacecraft had been used. Designers at NASA had taken a gamble whether or not it would work, and it paid off.

Shortly after the capsule settled on the red surface of the planet, the walls of the capsule unfolded like the petals of a flower to reveal its precious cargo—*Sojourner*. The small six-wheeled vehicle then automatically rolled out of the capsule.

Once free, the solar-powered and remote-controlled rover roamed the planet. As it trundled along, cameras on board took a stream of pictures that have thrilled the scientists back home.

THE LONER ROVER

While *Sojourner* set off to work, *Pathfinder* proved to be more than just pretty packaging—it's also a high-tech probe.

HAPPY LANDING: On impact with Mars, the *Pathfinder* lander opens up to release the remote-controlled *Sojourner*.

ON MARS!

Cameras on board took photos of *Sojourner*, while other instruments monitored the weather conditions on the planet.

Several billion nuggets of information have been sent back to Earth in the last two months — enough information for scientists to assess that future rovers can be bigger and travel greater distances on Mars.

There are no plans yet to land astronauts on the planet — the distances involved make it a tough mission to undertake. What scientists are prepared to say for now is that the day when humans walk on Mars will arrive. They're just not saying when. ☏

ON SAFARI: *Sojourner* takes in the sights of Mars.

ANYONE OUT THERE?

WITH THE WORLD focusing its attention on Mars, the embers of an age-old debate were relit. Once again scientists began to ponder the notion: could there ever have been life on Mars? *The History News* put that very question to two experts at opposite ends of the argument.

"IT'S UNLIKELY," said our first expert. "As everyone knows, the one thing that living organisms need for survival is water. And there isn't a drop of the stuff on Mars.

I'd have thought the recent glut of images of the planet that have filled our TV screens, courtesy of *Sojourner*, would have shattered that ludicrous Martian notion once and for all.

I mean, just look at the place — the whole planet is a desert! The temperature drops to –212°F at night. And it's ravaged by dust storms.

Ever since Lowell's madcap theory about the existence of intelligent beings on Mars, people have been obsessed with the idea that there's something out there. His theories were disproved almost a hundred years ago. And still people persist with the fantasy. That is not good science. When someone shows me proof of life on Mars, then, and only then, will I revise my opinion. But I doubt that will ever happen."

"IT'S POSSIBLE," said the second. "In fact, I think it's likely that life once did exist on Mars. There is frozen water at the planet's poles and strong evidence to suggest that much of the planet was once covered in water.

At that time, the climate may have been warm enough for the development of some primitive life forms in warm, dark oceans.

After all, that's what happened on Earth, and from what we know already about the planets, Mars appears to be the one most like ours. That is why I believe it happened there, too. You have to admit, it's possible!" ☏

GUESSING GAME: Was there ever life on Mars?

NOW WATCH THIS SPACE!

SINCE THE space age began in the 1950s, men have walked on the Moon, probes have been to every planet, and a car has traveled on the surface of Mars. Here, our space expert reveals what lies ahead.

NOW THAT THE rivalry between the USA and the USSR has ended, the most noticeable change affecting future space developments is the spirit of cooperation between Russia and the USA.

One particular project has brought together the two nations with the most experience of space—a new orbiting space station that would be permanently manned, due to be in operation by 2003.

The idea was initially developed by the USA, but in 1993 Russia agreed to join in and share the costs. The project has since become more of an international venture, with Canada, Japan, and many European countries involved.

ALL ABOARD THE SPACE SHIP

To ferry astronauts to and from the international space station and replace the shuttle, NASA is developing the *X-33*.

Unlike the first shuttles, it will have one engine that is completely reusable, with no need for external boosters.

The *X-33* will be more like a spaceplane than its predecessors. And once this super-efficient means

X-TRA SPECIAL: The *X-33* is the next step in space travel.

of space flight has been perfected, it won't be long before we see the first Moon bases.

The Moon would be an ideal platform for a telescope, and it's also much easier to launch a rocket in zero gravity than it is from Earth. The Moon is a perfect starting point from which to reach other planets.

Manned missions to Mars are on hold until the orbiting space station is up. And it will take at least 12 years from that time until the first astronaut lands on Mars.

As for visiting other planets, we have no evidence to show that any of them are suitable for manned landings, but their moons may be. Their main attraction for scientists is their wealth of minerals. It is hoped that Earth's dwindling mineral supplies might one day be replaced by new ones from space. For example, we know that there's helium on the Moon and water in comets, both of which are valuable resources.

Experts agree that the next chapter of the space age won't start until we have easy access to space. For this, we need a low-cost, reusable launch vehicle, which we are sure to have within 50 years.

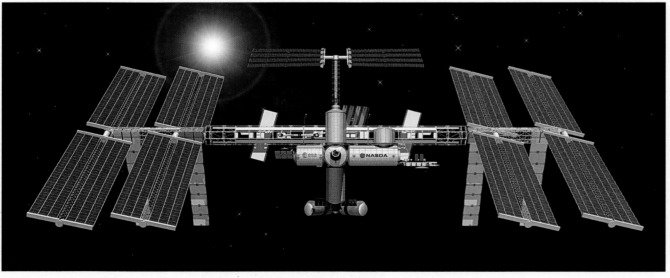

TOMORROW'S WORLD: Designing the international space station will take space technology into the next millennium.

TIME LINE

500 B.C.
Followers of Pythagoras teach that the Earth is round.

300 B.C.
Aristarchus of Samos states that all the planets revolve around the Sun.

A.D. 145
Ptolemy completes his famous book on Greek astronomy. In it, he states that the Earth is a sphere and all the other planets revolve around it.

1543
Copernicus publishes *De Revolutionibus*, in which he argues that the Earth and the other planets all revolve around the Sun.

1609
Johan Kepler publishes a book proving that the planets orbit the Sun in elliptical paths and do not go around in circles.

1633
Galileo Galilei is tried by the Church and found guilty of supporting the view that the Earth revolves around the Sun.

1682
Edmund Halley studies the comet that now bears his name.

1687
Isaac Newton publishes the *Principia*, in which he sets out his laws of motion and theory of gravity.

1733
William Herschel sights the planet Uranus.

1835
The Catholic Church lifts its ban on supporting the Copernican system.

1846
Johanne Galle discovers the planet Neptune.

1877
Giovanni Schiaparelli writes a book about "canali," or channels, on the surface of Mars.

1906
Percival Lowell publishes *Mars and Its Canals,* based on his reading of Schiaparelli's findings. He interprets the canals as being waterways built by alien beings.

1926
Robert Goddard launches the world's first liquid-propelled rocket.

1930
Clyde Tombaugh discovers the planet Pluto.

1933–45
In Germany, Wernher von Braun develops a new rocket program.

1945
World War II ends. Wernher von Braun and his team of missile experts surrender to US forces.

1957
USSR launches *Sputnik I* and later sends a dog named Laika into space.

1957
The USA attempt to launch its *Vanguard* satellite fails.

1961
The USSR sends the first man into space. Cosmonaut Yuri Gagarin orbits the Earth in *Vostok I.*

1963
Valentina Tereshkova of the USSR is the first woman to travel in space.

1965
USSR cosmonaut Aleksei Leonov makes the first space walk.

1966
Two US astronauts, Neil Armstrong and David Scott, make the first space docking in *Gemini 8.*

1967
After making a test flight in *Soyuz 1,* cosmonaut Vladimir Komarov is killed when his parachute fails to open.

1969
Astronauts Neil Armstrong and Edwin Aldrin of the US spacecraft *Apollo 11* land on the Moon.

1971
The USSR launches *Salyut* space station into orbit.

1977
The USA launches *Voyager 1* and *Voyager 2,* outer-solar-system probes.

1981
The US launches the space shuttle, the first reusable spacecraft.

1986
The US shuttle *Challenger* explodes just after lift-off, killing all seven people on board. Among the crew was school teacher Christa McAuliffe.

1990
The *Hubble Space Telescope,* or *HST,* is launched.

1993
The faulty optical lens of the *Hubble Space Telescope* is corrected while it is still in orbit.

1997
The US *Pathfinder* mission lands a roving camera on the surface of Mars.

Author: Michael
   Johnstone
Consultant:
   Doug Millard,
   Associate Curator of
   Space Technology at
   the Science Museum,
   London
Editor: Anderley Moore
Designer: Jonathan Hair

Ad illustrations by:
Jonathan Hair: 2t, 2c, 5,
   14bl
Karen Weinberg Goodman:
   11bl
Mike White: 7, 16bl, 17br

Small illustrations by:
Jonathan Hair: 3b, 6bl
Diane Lilley: 6tl, 9br
Richard Morris: 28b
Willie Ryan: 9bl, 9bm,
   23tr, 23mr, 23br
Karen Weinberg Goodman:
   14br, 31
Mike White: 9tr

With thanks to:
Artist Partners
Beehive Illustration
Jacqui Figgis
Folio
Hardlines
Illustration Limited
NASA
Temple Rogers

Text copyright © 1999 by
   Michael Johnstone
Illustrations copyright © 1999
   by Walker Books Ltd

All rights reserved.

First U.S. edition 1999

Johnstone, Michael.
The history news in space /
   Michael Johnstone,
   consultant, Douglas Millard.
   p. cm.
Includes index.
Summary: Uses a newspaper
   format to take a look at
   developments that led from the
   ideas of Copernicus and other
   early scientists to the
   technological advances that
   enabled man to venture to the
   moon and beyond.

ISBN 0-7637-0490-9

1. Astronautics—Juvenile
   literature. 2 Outer Space—
   Exploration—Juvenile
   literature. [1. Astronautics—
   History. 2. Outer Space—
   Exploration.] I. Title.
   TL793.J63 1999
   629.4—dc21 98-38682

2 4 6 8 10 9 7 5 3 1

Printed in Hong Kong

Candlewick Press
2067 Massachusetts Avenue
Cambridge, Massachusetts
02140

SOURCES

David Baker, *The Rocket*
Nicolaus Copernicus, *De Revolutionibus*
Galileo Galilei, *Dialogue on the Two Great
   Systems of the World*
Kenneth Gatland, *The Illustrated Encyclopedia
   of Space Technology*
James Harford, *Korolev*
Michael Hoskin, *The Cambridge Illustrated
   History of Astronomy*
Isaac Newton, *Principia Mathematica*
Ptolemy, *Almagest*
Frederick Ordway III and Mitchell Sharpe,
   The Rocket Team
Hugh Thurston, *Early Astronomy*
Peter Whitfield, *The Mapping of the Heavens*
Bill Yenne, *The Encyclopedia of US Spacecraft*
NASA website: http://www.nasa.gov